CAFFEINE
+
CELEBRATION

Steven Case

THE
PILGRIM
PRESS
Cleveland

This series is dedicated with respect, admiration, and gratitude to the youth of the Windermere Union Church who allowed me to try out many of these lessons in our meetings. Thank you. You made me better.

The Pilgrim Press, 700 Prospect Avenue, Cleveland, Ohio 44115-1100
thepilgrimpress.com
© 2008 by Steven Case

Scripture quotations, unless otherwise noted, are from the New Revised Standard Version of the Bible, © 1989 by the Division of Christian Education of the National Council of Churches of Christ in the United States of America and are used by permission. Changes have been made for inclusivity.

14   13   5   4   3   2

Library of Congress Cataloging-in-Publication Data

Case, Steve L., 1964-
  Caffeine and celebration / Steven Case.
      p. cm.
  ISBN-13: 978-0-8298-1846-8 (alk. paper)
  1. Church year--Study and teaching. 2. Fasts and feasts--Study and teaching. 3. Youth--Religious life--Study and teaching. 4. Church work with youth. I. Title.
  BV30.3.C355 2009
  268'.433--dc22
                            2009005363

CONTENTS

AULD LANG SYNE

THEME:
NEW YEAR'S DAY
ORDER HERE

New Year's Day is one of those holidays that lets us know we are human. We are all human. We all have failures and successes. We all have dreams and expectations. New Year's Day is the chance to say, "The past is over and done. Now let's see what happens next." It is a time of renewal and second chances (and third and fourth chances). It is a time of forgiveness and hope. It is our chance to believe that we can start over and make something out of the mess we made the previous year. It is a time to believe all things can be new. God has a very similar idea, only God calls it Grace.

START THINKING

Rank the following 1 to 10 according to their importance to you, with 1 meaning "Eh, not so much" and 10 meaning "Yeah, baby."

- First slice of pizza from the tray
- First one to read a fresh newspaper
- First kiss
- First alcoholic beverage
- First in line to see a movie
- First one to own the "it" (CD or video game)
- First one to know
- First one to get the "high score"
- First one to raise your hand when the teacher asks a question

TABLE NOTES

In the space below or on the back of a place mat, draw an old fashioned clock with the hands showing five minutes to midnight. Imagine it is almost midnight on New Years Eve. Write down exactly what you were doing at this time last year. Write down what you think you will be doing next New Year's Eve.

SCRIPTURE MENU

Look up the verses and ask the questions that follow.

Philippians 1:18–21 (MsgB)

So how am I to respond? I've decided that I really don't care about their motives, whether mixed, bad, or indifferent. Every time one of them opens his mouth, Christ is proclaimed, so I just cheer them on!

And I'm going to keep that celebration going because I know how it's going to turn out. Through your faithful prayers and the generous response of the Spirit of Jesus Christ, everything he wants to do in and through me will be done. I can hardly wait to continue on my course. I don't expect to be embarrassed in the least. On the contrary, everything happening to me in this jail only serves to make Christ more accurately known, regardless of whether I live or die. They didn't shut me up; they gave me a pulpit! Alive, I'm Christ's messenger; dead, I'm his bounty. Life versus even more life! I can't lose.

"They didn't shut me up; they gave me a pulpit!" What a wonderful line. What was the best thing that ever came out of a bad situation for you? Answer this both culturally and personally.

2 Corinthians 5:16–17 (NRSV)

16From now on, therefore, we regard no one from a human point of view; even though we once knew Christ from a human point of view, we know him no longer in that way. 17So if anyone is in Christ, there is a new creation: everything old has passed away; see, everything has become new!

There is a deep sense of hope in this passage. When we say, "Everything old is gone," do we really believe it? How much of our current problems are actually problems of which we refuse to let go?

What if your "baggage" really was baggage? What would you be carrying? How would you get around? How is it affecting you now?

Romans 8:29 (NRSV)

For those whom he foreknew he also predestined to be conformed to the image of his Son, in order that he might be the firstborn within a large family.

In the space below, in your journal, or on another sheet of paper, write down five outcomes that feel predestined in your life, perhaps by your parents, perhaps by God, perhaps by your situation in general. How would you prefer those aspects of your life to turn out? Which ones are you glad will probably turn out the way they were "predestined"?

_____

_____

_____

_____

_____

_____

Read Psalm 51:1–19 and 2 Samuel 12:19–20.
The Psalm was written about the time the events in the passage from 2 Samuel happened. Read them and decide which one came first. What if it were the other way around?

When the worst that can happen does happen, how long do you stay down?

How well do you turn the page in your life? Explain. If your answer is "depends," explain on what it depends.

What is your secret for "moving on"?

Read Nehemiah 2:17–18.

Then read John 3:5–6, Romans 8:16, and 2 Corinthians 4:6

All three passages refer to our need to connect with the absolute beginning—the moment when there was nothing and then there was everything. How do we symbolize the recognition of that moment? If all the energy that was there then is here now and it's in us, how do we show that? How do we let it dim?

Imagine the giant ball is dropping, and it will "light up" the New Year. Write down five "lights" for your new year—five areas that you are going to illuminate with God's help.

Take Home Bag

The song "Auld Lang Syne" is a toast "to the good old days" or "to old time's sake."

Write down the names of five people you haven't spoken to in five years or more. Focus yourself to think about them this week. Then before the next gathering contact them just to say "Hi."

Harry: "What does this song mean? My whole life I don't know what this songs means."

Sally: "Well, maybe it just means that we should remember that we forgot them or something. Anyway, it's about old friends."

—Billy Crystal and Meg Ryan as Harry and Sally in

When Harry Met Sally

THE LIGHT

THEME: EPIPHANY

ORDER HERE

Epiphany is the day in January when we celebrate the arrival of the wise men (kings? Magi?) who had come bearing gifts to pay homage to the baby Jesus. (He was probably four years old at the time. Really.) An "epiphany" is a "sudden realization" or a moment when "things are made clear." For the wise men, it was the sudden realization that the God who created the universe walks among us. That must have been *huge* for them. Since we've heard the stories and sang the songs for two thousand years, sometimes the shine can wear off the epiphany for us. That's why God is here to remind us...all the time.

START THINKING

Rate the following "realizations" on a scale from 1 to 10, with 1 meaning "Yeah? So?" and 10 meaning "HOLY CRAP!"

- Hey, mayonnaise really does go bad if you leave it out on the counter overnight.
- The three kings didn't show up at the stable?
- The Bible doesn't say there were *three* kings?
- The three kings weren't kings?
- The Bible doesn't call the kings by name?
- Mary Magdalene wasn't a prostitute?
- We have a test today?
- Wait—mom and dad "do it"?
- FICA took HOW MUCH out of my paycheck?

TABLE NOTES

Imagine you have a new camera—a magical camera that takes pictures of your life when you don't know about it. Problem: There's no automatic focus. In the space below or on the back of a place mat, draw three out-of-focus pictures of three areas of your life for which you can't quite get a clear picture.

SCRIPTURE MENU

Look up one or more of the sets of verses, and respond to the discussion questions that follow.

Matthew 2:1–2 (NRSV)

¹In the time of King Herod, after Jesus was born in Bethlehem village of Judea, wise men from the East came to Jerusalem, ²asking, "Where is the child who has been born king of the Jews? For we observed his star at its rising, and have come to pay him homage."

The Magi—an old term for the wise men—traveled for a very, very long time. They had prepared for the event but the realization of what was actually transpiring still blew them away. When was the last time you planned for something and still were not even close to fully prepared for what happened?

The Magi brought gold (money), frankincense (perfume), and myrrh (a gum resin used in preparing a body for burial). Giving the gift of myrrh is akin to bringing a coffin to a baby shower. What kind of gift was that?

Read Psalm 42:1–11.

Psalm 42 seems to include more than one voice. Break this psalm down by lines with two speakers. Who is saying what?

How does the psalmist's epiphany show up?

Would you rather have the "sudden realization" or a "slow understanding"?

Luke 15:11–32

11Then Jesus said, "There was a man who had two sons. 12The younger of them said to his father, 'Father, give me the share of the property that will belong to me.' So he divided his property between them. 13A few days later the younger son gathered all he had and traveled to a distant country, and there he squandered his property in dissolute living. 14When he had spent everything, a severe famine took place throughout that country, and he began to be in need."

Keep reading Luke 15 through verse 32.

In this passage from Luke, Jesus tells the story of the prodigal son. What was the young man's epiphany? Where did he have to be before he got it?

In your experience, does it seem like you have to be "dead" or "lost" before you finally have an epiphany?

Read these passages together.

2 Corinthians 4:5-6
Philippians 1:6
John 3:5-6

If you can't prepare for or study for an epiphany, how can you make yourself ready for one?

Think of the phrase "God is love." How many different ways can you imagine that phrase being an epiphany?

Talk about your favorite ride on a roller coaster. Now think of what that ride would have been like if you had spent your life never knowing there was such a thing as a roller coaster. We miss the epiphany of the Magi because we have always known

Jesus—not just hoped for him. What things in our lives do we use to "dull the shine"? How do you polish?

Take Home Bag

Do this activity before the next gathering. Using your cell phone, mirror, or any reflective surface, see if you catch the sunlight from the window and reflect it to a part of the room that never gets any light. This is bigger than a science experiment.

Tip

An artist's duty is rather to stay open-minded and in a state where he can receive information and inspiration. You always have to be ready for that little artistic Epiphany.

—Nick Cave

I GIVE UP

THEME: LENT

Disclaimer: Denominations vary on how they view Satan. We've looked at who or what Satan is or means in other Explorations. This Exploration uses the scriptures of Jesus' time in the wilderness when he was tempted by the devil. You might want to add to or adjust this lesson to match your church's beliefs.

ORDER HERE

The celebration or "season" of lent occurs for the forty days before Easter (excluding Sundays). Just as Easter moves around on the calendar, so does Lent. The word "lent" means "spring" and comes from the German word for "long"—as in the days are getting longer. The opening day of Lent is Ash Wednesday. On this day many Christian churches have special services in which ashes are "imposed" on people's foreheads by the clergy. These ashes come from burned palm branches from the previous year's Palm Sunday. It is a way of recognizing that Jesus went from being hailed as he entered Jerusalem to being put to death just one week later. The ashes symbolize abandonment. Not a happy holiday, but an important one.

START THINKING

Many of the ideas and traditions of the season of Lent come to us from when Jesus went into the desert to be alone and was tempted by Satan. The devil's "temptations" all dealt with Jesus' identity and who he believed himself to be. Let's start by thinking about identity.

Circle the words that are closest to the "you" that you are.
I am...

● My brother's keeper/ My own man or woman

- Just like my mother / father
- A dancer / A painter / A singer
- Order / Chaos
- A lover / A fighter
- Your worst nightmare / Your last best hope
- A legend in my own time / A legend in my own mind
- "Staying Alive" by the Bee Gees / "I Won't Back Down" by Tom Petty
- A Rock / Dust in the Wind
- Testing the Waters / Cannonball

TABLE NOTES

Which of these four makes you feel closer to God?

- Prayer—Communication with God through song, speech, meditation, or some other expression
- Penance—Repentance; doing something to make up for the rotten things you did since last Easter
- Abstinence—Self-denial of a vice; sacrificing as Jesus did in the wilderness
- Almsgiving—Giving to the poor in time, talent, or treasure

For the one you choose, create a symbol that could be imposed on the forehead in ashes.

SCRIPTURE MENU

Look up the verses and ask the questions that follow.

Genesis 3:17–19
Job 42:4–6

Does your church have more pictures of Jesus on the cross, Jesus teaching, Jesus with the children, or some other image? Why do you think this is so?

Without naming names, think about the person who is most likely to remind you that you are dust, nothing, or meaningless. Why do you value that person's opinion?

Can you be a dancer if you haven't crawled across the floor? (That's a metaphor.)

Lent, like Advent, is a time of preparing and remembering. Where do you go to "clear your head"? How in general do you get yourself to focus when the rest of the world is in chaos around you? How could you apply that to Lent? How could you teach it to someone else?

Read: Matthew 4:1–11
Mark 1:9–13
Luke 4:1–13

Notice that in all three mentions of this event in the life of Jesus, Satan (or the devil) tries to get under Jesus' skin by questioning his identity. He pushes all the buttons that say, "Oh yeah—you think you're so special?"

Perhaps the two greatest questions asked by teenagers around the world are "Who am I?" and "Where do I fit in?" Why are these questions so difficult? How do you answer them? Which is more important to you: who you are or whose you are?

Read Psalm 51:1–19.
This is one of David's most "penitent" Psalms. It was written after he slept with another man's wife and then had the husband killed. What does David acknowledge before God? What does David ask of God? What does David promise God? Find David's answers to these questions in Psalm 51. Pick

one sentence as example of an answer to each the questions and rewrite those sentences in your own words. Share your sentences with those around you.

Take Home Bag

Take a look at the choice you made under *Table Notes*. Draw the symbol on a napkin, the back of a place mat, or another sheet of paper. Put this in your wallet or on the mirror where you can read it in the morning. Let it be your reminder for the next forty days of how you connect with God.

Tip

The imposition of ashes is a dark and undeniable slash across your forehead, a bold proclamation of death and resurrection all at once. You forget that it is on your forehead and you walk out of church, out into the world, a living reminder that Christ died for us.

—*Lauren Winner*

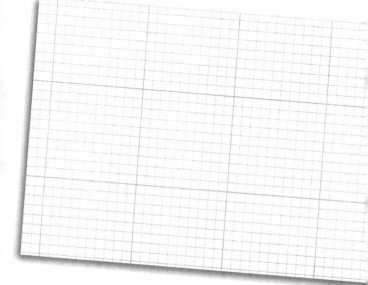

HEART TO HEART

Theme: SAINT VALENTINE'S DAY

ORDER HERE

Much of the history of Saint Valentine has been lost to the ages. It is generally accepted that Valentine was a priest who committed the crime against Rome of marrying Christian couples when that sort of thing had been forbidden. He was jailed but was released on occasion to come to the Emperor Claudius's dinner parties to debate Christianity for entertainment purposes. Apparently he tried to convert the emperor and was ordered to be beaten to death. When he stubbornly refused to die, he was beheaded. It was Pope Gelasius who declared February 14 to be Saint Valentine's Day. There is a legend that says the good priest cured the blindness of a prison guard's daughter (from his cell no less). He allegedly wrote a letter to the girl and signed it, "From your Valentine."

START THINKING

Roses Are Red, Violets Are Blue...

In the space below or on a separate sheet of paper, finish the poem for the following people:

Your boyfriend or girlfriend
Your best friend
Your youth minister
Your parents
A homeless guy on the corner
Jesus

TABLE NOTES

In the space below, in your journal, or on the back of a place mat, draw four hearts. Beneath each heart write one of the following.

EROS PHILLA STORGE AGAPE

Eros is passionate love, *philla* is brotherly love, *storge* is compassionate love, and *agape* is unconditional love. On each heart write the initials of someone who has shown you this love or to whom you have shown this love. (Note: If you don't want to fill in the "eros" heart, you can skip it.)

SCRIPTURE MENU

Look up one or more of the sets of verses, and respond to the discussion questions that follow.

1 John 4:7–8 (NIV)

⁷Dear friends, let us love one another, for love comes from God. Everyone who loves has been born of God and knows God. ⁸Whoever does not love does not know God, because God is love.

John writes that everyone who "loves" knows God. *Everyone.* Does this include atheists? People from other religions? People on death row? Is the act of "loving" all you need to be called a child of God?

Now look at the second part of this passage.

1 John 4:9–12 (NIV)

⁹This is how God showed his love among us: He sent his one and only Son into the world that we might live through him. ¹⁰This is love: not that we loved God, but that he loved us and sent his Son as an atoning sacrifice for our sins. ¹¹Dear friends, since God so loved us, we also ought to love one another. ¹²No one has ever seen God; but if we love one another, God lives in us and his love is made complete in us.

Do you think there are any restrictions on God's love? Explain.

1 Corinthians 13:1–7 (NRSV)

[1]**If I speak in the tongues of mortals and of angels, but do not have love, I am a noisy gong or a clanging cymbal. [2]And if I have prophetic powers, and understand all mysteries and all knowledge, and if I have all faith, so as to remove mountains, but do not have love, I am nothing. [3]If I give away all my possessions, and if I hand over my body so that I may boast, but do not have love, I gain nothing.**

[4]Love is patient; love is kind; love is not envious or boastful or arrogant [5]or rude. It does not insist on its own way; it is not irritable or resentful; [6]it does not rejoice in wrongdoing, but rejoices in the truth. [7]It bears all things, believes all things, hopes all things, endures all things.

When you watch the judges on TV talent shows, who do you like the most? Who would you least want to be judged by? How is some criticism like a clanging gong?

How is it possible to be "too smart for your own good?"

Name some ways in which we let our religion get in the way of our Christianity.

Is it possible to have faith and not love?

Look at the "Love is" section of 1 Corinthians 13. In the space below or on a separate sheet of paper, write these words: Patient, Kind, Humble, Polite, Selfless, Encouraging, Tolerant. Write them in the order of how well you show these to the world around you. Start with the one you need to work on the most.

Acts 4:32–35 (NRSV)

[32]**Now the whole group of those who believed were of one heart and soul, and no one claimed private ownership of any posses-**

sions, but everything they owned was held in common. [33]**With great power the apostles gave their testimony to the resurrection of the Lord Jesus, and great grace was upon them all.** [34]**There was not a needy person among them, for as many as owned lands or houses sold them and brought the proceeds of what was sold.** [35]**They laid it at the apostles' feet, and it was distributed to each as any had need.**

Song of Songs 1:12–14 (NIV)
[12]**While the king was at his table,
my perfume spread its fragrance.**
[13]**My lover is to me a sachet of myrrh
resting between my breasts.**
[14]**My lover is to me a cluster of henna blossoms
from the vineyards of En Gedi.**

This short passage from the Song of Songs is from the sexiest book in the scriptures. There are those who say that the Song of Songs is merely meta-phorical and that it's about God's love for his creation. Uhhh...maybe.

Why do some people have a problem with the Bible being "hot"?

If the Bible is a book that reveals universal truths, what's wrong with a book about two people who can't keep their hands off each other?

If God is love and love is God, are we in essence showing our love for God by passionately loving another person?

Take Home Bag

Using a sheet of paper or a place mat, tear out a heart shape. Pick one of the verses from the Scripture Menu, and write it on your heart. Leave the heart somewhere a random stranger will pick it up.

She gimme love, love, love, love, crazy love.

—*Van Morrison*

BIND

THEME: SAINT PATRICK'S DAY

ORDER HERE

There is not much physical evidence that allows any accurate knowledge of Saint Patrick. Some say there were two men named Patrick whose stories were combined along the way. There are two surviving letters written by Saint Patrick sometime before the year 487. We do know that he was captured when he was a teenager and taken to Ireland to be a slave. He escaped, returned home to England, and later returned to the same area of Ireland as a missionary. The story is told that in those days the Druid elders were the "keepers of fire"—if you wanted fire for your house you had to make the long journey to the Druid elders to get "fire" and take it back with you. Patrick, apparently looking for a good discussion starter, set up a bonfire halfway between the village and the Druid elders. He gave "fire" away and used the opportunity to tell others about Christ.

START THINKING

True or False?

1. Saint Patrick was Irish.
2. Patrick's given name was Maewyn Succat.
3. Saint Patrick wore green.
4. Saint Patrick used the shamrock as an object lesson for the Trinity.
5. Saint Patrick drove the snakes out of Ireland.

Answers: 1. False. He was born in Wales, His father was Italian. 2. True 3. False. He wore blue. 4. True 5. Up for grabs. Norsemen called him the remover of "toads." Some say that "toads" or "snakes" actually referred to the Druids.

TABLE NOTES

Draw a three-leaf clover in the space below or on the back of a place mat. Label the leaves Father, Son, and Holy Ghost. Make a list of five things in your life to which you must give your "whole self" to in order to be successful.

SCRIPTURE MENU

Instead of the usual scripture references for this Exploration, we'll look at what is commonly known as "Saint Patrick's Prayer," also called "The Shield of Saint Patrick" or "Saint Patrick's Breastplate." It has been shortened here for space reasons. You can find the complete prayer online at many Web sites by using an Internet search engine. Note that versions may vary in translation from the old Irish text.

Saint Patrick's Prayer
I bind myself today
To a strong virtue, an invocation of the Trinity.
I believe in a Threeness, with confession of an Oneness
In the Creator of the Universe.

I bind myself today to the virtue of ranks of Cherubim,
in obedience of Angels,
[in service of Archangels]
in hope of resurrection for reward,
in prayers of Patriarchs,
in preaching of Apostles,
in faiths of Confessors,
in innocence of Holy Virgins,
in deeds of righteous men.

I bind myself today to
The virtue of Heaven,
In light of Sun,
In brightness of Snow
In splendour of Fire,
In speed of Lightning,
In swiftness of Wind,
In depth of Sea,
In stability of Earth,
In compactness of Rock.

I bind myself today to
God's Virtue to pilot me,
God's might to uphold me,
God's wisdom to guide me,
God's eye to look before me,
God's ear to hear me,
God''s word to speak to me,
God's hand to guard me,
God's way to lie before me,
God's shield to protect me,
God's host to secure me,
Against snares of demons,
Against seductions of vices,
Against lusts of nature,
Against every one who wishes ill to me,
Afar and anear,
Alone and in a multitude.

Christ with me, Christ before me,
Christ behind me, Christ in me!
Christ below me, Christ above me.
Christ at my right, Christ at my left!
Christ in breadth, Christ in length, Christ in height!
Christ in the heart of everyone who thinks of me,
Christ in the mouth of everyone who speaks to me,
Christ in every eye that sees me,
Christ in every ear that hears me!

I bind myself today
To a strong virtue, an invocation of the Trinity.

I believe in a Threeness with confession of a Oneness,
In the Creator of the Universe.
Salvation is the Lord's, salvation is the Lord's,
Salvation is Christ's
May Thy salvation, O Lord, be always with us.

To what do you "bind" yourself?

Of the environmental topics mentioned in Saint Patrick's Prayer—Sun, Snow, Fire, Lightning, Wind, Sea, Earth, Rock—which one most closely represents your faith at this point in your life? Has it changed in the last few years? In what way could one of the others be a goal to you?

Patrick asks for God's hand, eye, ear, might, wisdom and word to be with him. Yet, he wants Christ to be in eyes, ears, and other places of those who see him (Patrick). What do you think this means?

If we really are Christ on this earth, if God is here because we are here, then how do we come to be "above," "below," and "beside" others?

Look at the section where Patrick talks about binding himself to the obedience of angels. Fill in your own ideas to this stanza. What group or individuals fit best for you in today's culture?

Take Home Bag

On a napkin, the back of place mat, or another sheet of paper, draw the outline of a flame. Tear this out and write one of the lines from the prayer. Keep this with you and give it out to someone randomly this week.

Before I was humiliated I was like a stone that lies in deep mud, and he who is mighty came and in his compassion raised me up and exalted me very high and placed me on the top of the wall.

—Saint Patrick

RAM-A-LAMB

Theme: PASSOVER (PESACH)

Order Here

Passover—or Pesach, as it is called in Hebrew—is one of the major holidays of the Jewish calendar. It usually takes place in the spring and is a one-day celebration immediately followed by the Festival of Unleavened Bread. The story goes that after Moses tried repeatedly to tell the pharaoh to release his people from slavery, God sent ten plagues on Egypt, the last of which was death to all the firstborn sons of every house. God told Moses to slaughter a lamb and to put blood on the doorways of all of the Jewish people's homes and then the angel of death would "pass over" those homes and those firstborns would be spared. It was this plague (and the loss of the pharaoh's own son) that finally got the message through to the pharaoh and persuaded him to let the people go.

Start Thinking

Make a list of ten plagues of modern times. Examples include telemarketers and computer viruses. It's okay to be funny (visualize raining frogs!), but remember that this ends with the deaths of hundreds of children.

TABLE NOTES

Using your pencil, a marker, or maybe lipstick (if you have any), color the tips of your fingers and leave four or five finger prints in the space below or on the back of a place mat.

SCRIPTURE MENU

Look up the verses and ask the questions that follow.

Exodus 12:6–13 (NRSV)

⁶You shall keep it until the fourteenth day of this month; then the whole assembled congregation of Israel shall slaughter it at twilight. ⁷They shall take some of the blood and put it on the two doorposts and the lintel of the houses in which they eat it. ⁸They shall eat the lamb that same night; they shall eat it roasted over the fire with unleavened bread and bitter herbs. ⁹Do not eat any of it raw or boiled in water, but roasted over the fire, with its head, legs, and inner organs. ¹⁰You shall let none of it remain until the morning; anything that remains until the morning you shall burn. ¹¹This is how you shall eat it: your loins girded, your sandals on your feet, and your staff in your hand; and you shall eat it hurriedly. It is the passover of the Lord. ¹²For I will pass through the land of Egypt that night, and I will strike down every firstborn in the land of Egypt, both human beings and animals; on all the gods of Egypt I will execute judgments: I am the Lord. ¹³The blood shall be a sign for you on the houses where you live: when I see the blood, I will pass over you, and no plague shall destroy you when I strike the land of Egypt.

What significance does this passage take on when we recall that Jesus is called the Lamb of God?

The notion of eating while wearing your travel clothes and eating unleavened bread (or made without yeast—much quicker to make) was a sign of the Israelites' faith. They knew they were going to be freed. Perhaps we can compare this to the night before Christmas or the night before a family vacation or the night before the first day of school. How do you feel on these nights? Do you sleep? Have you ever intentionally slept in the clothes you will be wearing the next day? Why?

Matthew 26:17–20 (NIV)

¹⁷On the first day of the Feast of Unleavened Bread, the disciples came to Jesus and asked, "Where do you want us to make preparations for you to eat the Passover?" ¹⁸He replied, "Go into the city to a certain man and tell him, 'The Teacher says: My appointed time is near. I am going to celebrate the Passover with my disciples at your house.'" ¹⁹So the disciples did as Jesus had directed them and prepared the Passover.

²⁰When evening came, Jesus was reclining at the table with the Twelve.

The Passover meal, called the Seder, is a meal with complicated rituals and readings. Seder involves very specific foods, and each taste has special significance. For example, the taste of saltwater recalls the tears shed by the Israelites. Can you think of food that people in your family or your church eat that has special significance in your life?

Is there a food that represents "Christmas" to you? Easter?

What are the stories that are told every year around your table?

Jesus was celebrating Passover with the Seder meal on the night he was arrested. What we think of as Communion, or Eucharist, began with the bread and wine left over after the Seder meal. What is the most meaningful food you eat (not your favorite food, but the most meaningful)? What food or taste connects with your past? Your future?

Read Psalm 111:1–10 and then Psalm 81:1–16.

In Jesus' time it was a tradition to sing Psalms after the Passover meal. It's likely that Psalm 81 and 111 were written for this purpose. Look at these two psalms. What connection do they have to the Seder? What song connects you to God?

Take Home Bag

What is the most religious symbol you know? (It doesn't have to be a cross.) Draw it in the space below or on a separate sheet of paper. If what you believe is the "most sacred" part of your faith has no symbol, make one up. Draw this symbol somewhere else before the next gathering, perhaps using sidewalk chalk in front of your school, on a test paper, in an art project. Talk about what you did at the next gathering.

Tip

Passover is one of my favorite times of the year. This is when the whole community and family gets together to remember who we are and why we are here.

—Jennifer Wagner

HERE WE ARE NOW

THEME: NIRVANA

ORDER HERE

Nirvana Day is the day on which Buddhists celebrate the death of Buddha. They do not celebrate his death as such. Buddha, it is believed, achieved complete enlightenment, called Nirvana, meaning perfect peace and an end to all want and suffering. Celebrations vary throughout the world. Some Buddhists treat it as a social occasion with food and gifts. Others use it a time of reflection on those who have died and what they themselves can do to achieve Nirvana.

START THINKING

Make a list of five gifts and five foods that you would give/ serve to celebrate total peace and oneness. (No fair saying "Pizza—make me one with everything.")

TABLE NOTES

One of the Four Noble Truths of Buddhism is to end suffering through what is called The Eightfold Path.

The Eightfold Path

1. Right view
2. Right intention
3. Right speech
4. Right action
5. Right livelihood
6. Right effort
7. Right mindfulness
8. Right contemplation

Look at the list of the eight aspects of the eightfold path. For each, describe a corresponding action that comes to mind.

SCRIPTURE MENU

Look up one or more of the sets of verses, and respond to the discussion questions that follow.

Matthew 14:22–23 (NRSV)

²²Immediately he made the disciples get into the boat and go on ahead to the other side, while he dismissed the crowds. ²³And after he had dismissed the crowds, he went up the mountain by himself to pray. When evening came, he was there alone....

John 6:14–15 (NRSV)

[14]When the people saw the sign that he had done, they began to say, "This is indeed the prophet who is to come into the world."

[15]When Jesus realized that they were about to come and take him by force to make him king, he withdrew again to the mountain by himself.

Luke 4:42–43 (NRSV)

[42]At daybreak he departed and went into a deserted place. And the crowds were looking for him; and when they reached him, they wanted to prevent him from leaving them. [43]But he said to them, "I must proclaim the good news of the kingdom of God to the other cities also; for I was sent for this purpose."

Luke 5:16 (MSGB)

As often as possible Jesus withdrew to out-of-the-way places for prayer.

Did Jesus meditate? What do you think the difference is between meditation and prayer?

The Ten Virtuous Acts of Buddhism

1. One must not kill.
2. One must not steal.
3. One must not engage in sexual misconduct.
4. One must not lie.
5. One must not defame others.
6. One must not engage in frivolous conversation out of conflicting emotions.
7. Do not speak offensive words.
8. Do not develop covetousness.
9. Do not hold malice.
10. Do not hold views that deny spiritual perfection.

Do these sound familiar? Look up the Ten Commandments (Exodus 20:1-17) and make a comparison.

What were Jesus' top two Commandments?

Nirvana is achieved when one has eliminated suffering from one's life. Buddhists meditate on the Four Noble Truths given to them by Buddha himself.

The Four Noble Truths
1. **Life is suffering.**
2. **Suffering is due to having desires.**
3. **Suffering ends when we overcome our desires.**
4. **We overcome desires when we follow the Eightfold Path.**

Is heaven similar to Nirvana? Do we have "Heaven Day"? If you don't think we do, should we? How would you celebrate it?

Matthew 25:34–40 (NRSV)

[34]**"Then the king will say to those at his right hand, 'Come, you that are blessed by my Father, inherit the kingdom prepared for you from the foundation of the world;** [35]**for I was hungry and you gave me food, I was thirsty and you gave me something to drink, I was a stranger and you welcomed me,** [36]**I was naked and you gave me clothing, I was sick and you took care of me, I was in prison and you visited me.'** [37]**Then the righteous will answer him, 'Lord, when was it that we saw you hungry and gave you food, or thirsty and gave you something to drink?** [38]**And when was it that we saw you a stranger and welcomed you, or naked and gave you clothing?** [39]**And when was it that we saw you sick or in prison and visited you?'** [40]**And the king will answer them, 'Truly I tell you, just as you did it to one of the least of these who are members of my family, you did it to me.'"**

In Buddhism, There is an emphasis on minimizing our own wants and needs, because wants and needs can cause suffering. In Christianity, one of the goals is to minimize suffering by meeting the needs of others.

Take Home Bag

*

Tip

Do not dwell in the past, do not dream of the future, concentrate the mind on the present moment.

—Buddha

*This is a pun. Get it?

IN THE MOURNING

THEME: MAUNDY THURSDAY

ORDER HERE

Maundy Thursday is the day we remember what is commonly known as The Last Supper, or the Eucharist.

The "last supper" was probably eaten off a table about two feet high with the disciples lying around the table on pillows. It was the Passover celebration, so there would have been food and singing and probably jokes and laughter. There was also the deep symbolism of the Seder, and communion was done for the very first time. The word Maundy comes from the Latin word *maundatum*, which means "mandate" or "command." Jesus gave the disciples his command: "Love each other."

START THINKING

Rate the following "commands" from 1 to 10, with 1 meaning "I think that's optional" and 10 meaning "Like my life depends on it."

- Obey the stop sign
- Do homework
- Do weekend homework
- Meet college application deadlines

- Punch the workplace time clock
- Remember your mother's birthday
- Go to church on Sunday
- Attend Youth Group meetings
- Flush
- Tip
- Recycle
- Do not take the Lord's name in vain
- No one under 17 admitted
- Rated M for mature

TABLE NOTES

Indiana Jones went in search of the Cup of Christ. There is a church in Rome that claims to have a finger bone of Saint John. In the space below or on a separate sheet of paper, make a list of all the holy relics you can think of. (No, not your senior pastor.)

SCRIPTURE MENU

Look up the verses and ask the questions that follow.

As you read or listen to these words from Exodus, remember that Jesus sat on the floor and listened to someone read them or maybe he read them himself. Imagine Jesus' voice as you read or listen.

Read Exodus 12:1–14.

How come we forget that Jesus was not Christian?

Why do some people have trouble with the idea that Jesus celebrated all of the Jewish ceremonies just like any other Jewish man in his time? Are we possessive of Jesus?

Have you ever pictured Jesus singing? Laughing? Passing gas?

Do we want our Jesus to be more human?

Read Psalm 78:1–72.

Psalm 78 is kind of depressing, isn't it? So why do you think this would be read at a worship service? What is the message to be taught here? How well do we learn that lesson as Christians and as humans?

Read Matthew 26:17–24.

Jesus gave his disciples a ritual (communion). We pretty much do it today exactly the same way as Jesus did. We add fancy stuff, but the breaking of bread and the tasting of wine are the way Jesus did it. That's a gift to us from Jesus so that we come to know him.

Imagine you had nothing, literally nothing, and you wanted to give someone a goodbye gift. What would you give?

Let's say you've been asked to create a representation of Jesus (a painting, a sculpture, a song, whatever) and you knew your work was going to be around for thousands of years. What do you think you would do? Where would you start?

Read John 13:3–14.

What was Jesus trying to teach the disciples? What's the problem with being in charge? How would you feel if you saw your teacher waiting tables?

John 13:15–17 (NRSV)

[15]For I have set you an example, that you also should do as I have done to you. [16]Very truly, I tell you, servants are not greater than their master, nor are messengers greater than the one who sent them. [17]If you know these things, you are blessed if you do them.

This is God we're talking about here. God. God in human form. God in flesh and blood. God on his knees scraping out the gunk from between your toes. Why would God do that? What is the message here? How would you teach that?

John 13:34–35 (NRSV)

[34]"I give you a new commandment, that you love one another. Just as I have loved you, you also should love one another. [35]By this everyone will know that you are my disciples, if you have love for one another."

This is the mandate—the *maundatum* (hence Maundy Thursday). Jesus' command to his disciples is that they "love each other." This is how we are recognized by the world as being Christians. How are we doing so far?

Take Home Bag

If you are sitting in a coffee shop, have a quick communion service with whatever is left on the table (that's how Jesus did it). Before the next gathering, break bread (have a meal) with someone and talk about your faith.

And they'll know we are Christians by our love, by our love / They will know we are Christians by our love.

—Peter Scholtes, "They'll Know We Are Christians by Our Love."

GOD'S

THEME: GOOD FRIDAY

ORDER HERE

"Oh yeah? What was so 'good' about it?" That's a question asked a lot. The answer is that it wasn't a "good" Friday—it was God's Friday. Most of the celebrations we have for Good Friday come to us from the Germans, who when saying "God's Friday" would pronounce God like "got" (*Gott*).

No, it wasn't a good Friday for Jesus or Mary or his disciples. It wasn't good, but it was necessary. Perhaps horrific is a better word. The death had to be horrific. It had to be the worst it could be. It had to be public or the resurrection would have been meaningless. Jesus had to die in the most horrible way possible so that his "coming back" could become world changing. Sometimes in the colors and smells and tastes and sounds of Easter morning we forget the bitterness, the blood, and the cave of Good Friday.

START THINKING

Circle one. I am...

- Green Day / It's Not Easy Being Green
- Johnny Cash / Pink
- David Blaine / David Copperfield
- The Dark Knight / Superman
- Sunrise / Sunset
- Full Moon / Blue Sky
- Dark chocolate M&Ms / Skittles

TABLE NOTES

Make two lists of five items each, one of "Intense Tastes"
and another of "Tastes That Could Follow." The first two
items in each list have been provided for you.

Intense Tastes
Five-alarm chili
Really fudgy brownies

Tastes That Could Follow
Ice-cold soda pop
Glass of milk

SCRIPTURE MENU

Look up one or more of the sets of verses, and respond to the
discussion questions that follow.

John 1:29–30 (NRSV)

²⁹**The next day he saw Jesus coming towards him and declared,**
"Here is the Lamb of God who takes away the sin of the world!
³⁰**This is he of whom I said, 'After me comes a man who ranks**
ahead of me because he was before me.'"

Given what you have learned about Passover, what would you think about being greeted this way?

John and Jesus had probably known each other since they were children. John became a screaming street-corner preacher who was gaining a large following. What was he telling the crowd? Why do you think Jesus wanted to begin his ministry this way?

Read Matthew 27:1–5.

Mark 15:1–3 (NRSV)

¹As soon as it was morning, the chief priests held a consultation with the elders and scribes and the whole council. They bound Jesus, led him away, and handed him over to Pilate. ²Pilate asked him, "Are you the King of the Jews?" He answered him, "You say so." ³Then the chief priests accused him of many things.

Mark 15:33–37 (MsgB)

At noon the sky became extremely dark. The darkness lasted three hours. At three o'clock, Jesus groaned out of the depths, crying loudly, "*Eloi, Eloi, lama sabachthani?*" which means, "My God, my God, why have you abandoned me?"

Some of the bystanders who heard him said, "Listen, he's calling for Elijah." Someone ran off, soaked a sponge in sour wine, put it on a stick, and gave it to him to drink, saying, "Let's see if Elijah comes to take him down."

But Jesus, with a loud cry, gave his last breath.

There are different ways that Good Friday has been studied and different lessons that came from it. Generations were taught that what occurred on Good Friday was proof that hatred of the Jewish people was justified. Bigotry and idiocy went hand in hand. Some say we should use the events of Good Friday to appreciate the good things that came from it rather than dwell on the pain and suffering.

Some theologians say the "take away" from this is to focus on the fact that God loved *us* so much that he allowed Good Friday to happen. Maybe we should consider that Jesus could have stopped it at anytime. Good Friday was his choice.

Which idea or lesson hits home with you? Which do you identify with the most? Is there one that you think hasn't been mentioned? Share your thoughts with the group.

TAKE HOME BAG

What is the longest you can go wearing a blindfold? Try wearing one for a length of time (you may need to get some help with this). You don't have to try and complete your normal day. Just sit in your own darkness.

Write the number of minutes (hours) you lasted here: _____

Write the first word(s) you thought when you took the blindfold off here: _____

How did that experience change your attitude toward the light?

TIP

Since the day He was born, there has been only ONE day that Jesus has not been with us.

—Allison Baker

ROLLING STONE

THEME: EASTER

ORDER HERE

This is our biggie. Jesus was born on Christmas, but it was on Easter that he came back from the dead. Until then there was always some doubt with some people (Hello? Thomas?) But, then, *the guy came back from the dead.* Commercially, Easter is about spring and renewal and flowers and sunshine. It's about the return of the sun (Son?). It's about new life and pastel M&Ms. Biblically, it's when the women in Jesus' life went to the tomb to prepare his dead body. And the tomb was empty. That's where it all really started, the reason you are sitting here now reading this book, the reason you have what you have and you are what you are. All of that was influenced directly and indirectly because the women went to the tomb and the tomb was empty.

START THINKING

The following is a list of actual products. Mark each one from 1 to 10 according to your own personal taste, with 10 meaning "that's acceptable" and 1 meaning "that's out of line."

- A chocolate Jesus head (complete with nuts)
- A chocolate cross
- A fluffy Easter bunny toy looking sad and holding a cross
- A "jumping Jesus"—a spring-loaded toy that jumps after you push it down
- A "Happy Easter" paddle ball set
- The image of three crosses on a hill printed on a day-glow Slinky
- A Happy Easter rubber wrist bracelet
- Jelly beans with crosses printed on them

TABLE NOTES

In the space below or on a napkin or the back of a place mat, take 60 seconds to make a list of all the things you can find in a garden. Don't just list vegetables. A few examples will start you out.

Seeds
Light
Water
Soil

Now go back and think of a biblical analogy for each word.

Seeds = Jesus was buried but he "grew."
Light = God's love
Water = Jesus said he was "living water."
Soil = Our foundation

SCRIPTURE MENU

Read the next four scripture passages together before discussing with your group:

Matthew 28:1-4
Mark 16:1-5
Luke 24:1-12

John 20:1–16 (NRSV)

¹Early on the first day of the week, while it was still dark, Mary Magdalene came to the tomb and saw that the stone had been removed from the tomb. ²So she ran and went to Simon Peter and the other disciple, the one whom Jesus loved, and said to them, "They have taken the Lord out of the tomb, and we do not know where they have laid him." ³Then Peter and the other disciple set out and went towards the tomb. ⁴The two were running together, but the other disciple outran Peter and reached the tomb first. ⁵He bent down to look in and saw the linen wrappings lying there, but he did not go in. ⁶Then Simon Peter came, following him, and went into the tomb. He saw the linen wrappings lying there, ⁷and the cloth that had been on Jesus' head, not lying with the linen wrappings but rolled up in a place by itself. ⁸Then the other disciple, who reached the tomb first, also went in, and he saw and believed; ⁹for as yet they did not understand the scripture, that he must rise from the dead. ¹⁰Then the disciples returned to their homes.

¹¹But Mary stood weeping outside the tomb. As she wept, she bent over to look into the tomb; ¹²and she saw two angels in white, sitting where the body of Jesus had been lying, one at the head and the other at the feet. ¹³They said to her, "Woman, why are you weeping?" She said to them, "They have taken away my Lord, and I do not know where they have laid him." ¹⁴When she had said this, she turned round and saw Jesus standing there, but she did not know that it was Jesus. ¹⁵Jesus said to her, "Woman, why are you weeping? For whom are you looking?" Supposing him to be the gardener, she said to him, "Sir, if you have carried him away, tell me where you have laid him, and I will take him away." ¹⁶Jesus said to her, "Mary!" She turned and said to him in Hebrew, "Rabbouni!" (which means Teacher).

Keep reading John 20 through verse 31.

Mary and the other women went to the tomb to fulfill their obligation according to Jewish law. There were certain rituals that had to be carried out. Does this show a lack of faith?

A minister by the name of Mike Yaconelli once said, "I wish the gospel ended with the finding of the empty tomb and Mary running away screaming." How would that have made things different? How would our faith be different if the gospels had ended there?

Read Acts 2:22–25.
This probably could be considered one of the first Christian sermons (in a sense). Peter is speaking to a crowd, and he begins to quote Psalm 16.

Read Psalm 16:1–11.

What does this Psalm have to do with Easter? What is the Easter "message" here? Is it still the only message?

Take Home Bag

Thinking as creatively (humorously or seriously) as you can—JESUS RISES FROM THE TOMB and THE HARD BOILED EASTER EGG.

Ready?

Go.

Sally: I don't believe it. It's Easter and they already have the Christmas decorations up.
Charlie: Good grief.

—Charlie Brown cartoon, "It's the Easter Beagle"

CHANCES

THEME: ROSH HASHANAH

ORDER HERE

Rosh Hashanah is a celebration of the Jewish New Year, usually held around the middle of September. Rosh Hashanah also celebrates the creation. It's not just about a New Year; it recognizes that with this celebration everything is brand new, as if there were no history before this moment. Rosh Hashanah is considered a day of rest. For many it is considered a day of judgment in which the "books of account" are opened. You can have your name written in the book of life, or are given ten days to turn your act around, or are erased from the books completely. A ram's horn is often blown to "wake up" those who have been lax in their relationships with God and their fellow humans.

START THINKING

Circle One.

- *Free samples:* Take one / Take one and one for a friend / Take a fistful / Take a pocket of them
- *Flat tire:* Stop and help / Oh that's too bad / One less idiot on the road
- *Homework:* A chance to learn / A kid with a C can tutor a kid with a C– / A necessary evil
- *Ice cream:* Two spoons please / Brain freeze / Smack a kid's hand and he'll drop his in the dirt

- *Servers:* Thank you / You want to hurry it up? / What's 7 percent of $4.50?
- *Someone falls in the hall:* Help them up / Laugh like crazy and then help them up / I didn't trip them—nope, wasn't me—can't prove anything
- *Waking up:* Pass me the horn, I've been up for hours / Holy crap what time is it? / Zzzzzzz

TABLE NOTES

In the space below, in your journal, or on the back of a place mat, list five people against whom you hold a grudge or who hold a grudge against you.

Imagine you have ten days to make it right or next year is really going to suck for you. What would you do first?

SCRIPTURE MENU

Read Psalm 81:1–16.

Psalm 81 was a song written by David probably for a New Year's party of some sort. It was more than likely sung and then taught to a large crowd of people. What conclusions could you come to about King David from this writing?

Is it comforting or does it make you uncomfortable to think that "people get what's coming to them"?

Would you welcome a chance every year to have ten days to make things right with those relationships in your life that are less than healthy?

On the secular New Year that we celebrate on January 1, what are some traditions you can name? Are any of them "sacred" in the biblical sense?

Do you believe there is a "Book of Life" of some kind, and someone, somewhere is keeping track of all the wrongs and rights of everyone in the world? Have you ever envisioned some kind of judgment when you get to heaven's gates?

Leviticus 23:23–25 (NRSV)

23The Lord spoke to Moses, saying: 24Speak to the people of Israel, saying: In the seventh month, on the first day of the month, you shall observe a day of complete rest, a holy convocation commemorated with trumpet blasts. 25You shall not work at your occupations; and you shall present the Lord's offering by fire.

How do you wake up in the morning? Are you more of an "up-and-at-'em" kind of person or a "snooze alarm" kind of person? Expand this so you are thinking about your life. How do you "wake up!"?

Read Numbers 29:1–40.

What is the most "intricate" holiday you are involved in? What would happen if we celebrated Christmas without a tree? What would happen if you didn't have the three wise men come to the stable in the Christmas pageant?

Read Psalm 69:1–36.

David was on the opposite end of the celebration in this Psalm. How easy is it for you to say, "I screwed up"? (Let's assume you did—how easy is it to admit it?)

Do you apologize well?

How well to you accept an apology?

Who holds grudges longer, men or women? Why do you think so?

There's a belief that what you are doing at midnight on New Year's Eve is symbolic for what your year will be like. How's that working for you so far?

Take Home Bag

*The traditional greeting on Rosh Hashanah is **shana tova** (SHAH-nah-TOH-vah), which means "blessed and sweet year." Or you may say **ketiva ve-chatima tovah**, which means "may your name be written and sealed for a good year."*

It is a tradition in some Rosh Hashanah celebrations to gather and pray near open water and throw small rocks on bread into the water to symbolize the casting off of sins. If you are meeting in a coffee shop, scrape the crumbs from the table and step outside to throw these into the parking lot. If you are in a classroom, improvise.

Tip

Ketiva ve-chatima tovah.
May your name be written and sealed for a good year.

CLEARING HOUSE
Theme: RAMADAN

Order Here

Ramadan is the Muslim religious observance of a 30-day period in which people are called to fast, study, cleanse, and purify themselves to bring them closer to God. In the Muslim faith it is the time in which God revealed the Qur'an to the prophet Mohammad. Muslims do not eat or drink from sunup to sundown. It is an opportunity for reflection and study and to express gratitude to Allah for his presence and his direction. It is a time of prayer asking for forgiveness of past sins and for help in refraining from everyday evils. Ramadan is intended to create a link between prayer and God through charity, good deeds, and kindness.

Start Thinking

Circle one. Yes, these are odd choices, but which one—right now—is closer to what you feel like?
I am...

- A window / A door
- Finger paint / Windex
- A hammer / A cement trowel
- Smoke / A fan
- Dental floss / DAP filler putty
- An empty ice cream container / A full can of bug spray
- A magnet / Teflon
- A storm drain / A puddle

TABLE NOTES

In the space below or on a separate piece of paper, draw a simple set of pipes, like you would see under your sink if you opened the cupboard door. Draw a big clog in the pipes at one of the bends. This set of pipes is your life. Happiness and contentment flow through the pipes, except that over time a clog (problem) has developed. List between five and ten things that make up that clog.

START THINKING

Look up the verses and ask the questions that follow.

2 Chronicles 20:1–4 (NRSV)

¹**After this the Moabites and Ammonites, and with them some of the Meunites, came against Jehoshaphat for battle. ²Messengers came and told Jehoshaphat, "A great multitude is coming against you from Edom, from beyond the sea; already they are at Hazazon-tamar" (that is, En-gedi). ³Jehoshaphat was afraid; he set himself to seek the Lord, and proclaimed a fast throughout all Judah. ⁴Judah assembled to seek help from the Lord; from all the towns of Judah they came to seek the Lord.**

"HEY JOE, there's a vast horde of deadly soldiers over the hill! They'll be here in days! What do we do?"

"Pray," says Joe.

The king called on his entire kingdom to fast, to take a break from work, to focus themselves. When was the last time you felt your country (as a people) was focused and thinking clearly together?

Joel 1:14 (MsgB)

Declare a holy fast, call a special meeting, get the leaders together, Round up everyone in the country. Get them into God's Sanctuary for serious prayer to God.

How hungry have you ever been? Does hunger clear you head?

How does a large group of people doing the same thing change the attitude about what one person is doing? Consider this example: A few days after John Lennon was shot his widow asked all stations that play his music to go silent for ten minutes. Thousands of stations that make a living off of sound went quiet.

Think of when you go to a concert and everyone stands and sings along with the encore, with their lighters or cell phones in the air. How is that different from hearing the same music on your iPod?

Read Matthew 6:6–9.

Fasting is incredibly difficult. Fasting is mandatory for the Jewish people on Yom Kippur. It gives people time to pray, it teaches self-discipline and reminds us that we can live on less. How is that important?

Can you think of any Christian holidays that require any kind of behavior to clear one's head?

How do you clear your head when your "pipes" get "clogged"?

Read the following passages together.

Mark 1:12-13
2 Timothy 4:3-5
2 Corinthians 4:16-18

Create a "Day of Head Clearing." Use any of the scriptures in this Exploration. Use Psalm 1, 19, or 51 as a prayer. What event from the Bible stories would you use as a basis? How long should the "time" be? Should it include fasting? For what purpose?

Will you link it to another Christian holiday or is this holiday completely separate? Take a few minutes as a group and see what you come up with.

Read Psalm 51:6–15.

Meditation is obedient reflection on God's Word. Many people think that prosperity and success come from having power, influential personal contacts, and a relentless desire to get ahead. But the strategy for gaining prosperity that God taught Joshua goes against such criteria. He said that to succeed, Joshua must (1) be strong and courageous because the task ahead would not be easy, (2) obey God's law, and (3) constantly read and study the Book of the Law—God's Word.

To be successful, follow God's words to Joshua. You may not succeed by the world's standards, but you will be a success in God's eyes—and God's commendation lasts forever.

Psalm 1:2 (MsgB)
[You] thrill to God's Word,
you chew on Scripture day and night.

Psalm 19:1–6 (NRSV)
¹The heavens are telling the glory of God;
and the firmament proclaims his handiwork.
²Day to day pours forth speech,
and night to night declares knowledge.
³There is no speech, nor are there words;
their voice is not heard;
⁴yet their voice goes out through all the earth,
and their words to the end of the world.

In the heavens he has set a tent for the sun,
⁵which comes out like a bridegroom from his wedding canopy,
and like a strong man runs its course with joy.
⁶Its rising is from the end of the heavens,
and its circuit to the end of them;
and nothing is hidden from its heat.

Take Home Bag

Imagine you have an actual paper bag in front of you. Instead of leftover food, there is a bit of nourishment that is mental (or emotional or spiritual). It's just a piece of advice that strengthens you. What would you write?

Share that with someone this week.

Tip

Why do they call it a fast when it goes so damn slow?

—Gallagher

I THINK IT'S
ABOUT FORGIVENESS

THEME: YOM KIPPUR
(THE DAY OF ATONEMENT)

ORDER HERE

Yom Kippur is a day of strict fasting, no food or drink, and often no bathing, perfumes, or sexual relations. The day before Yom Kippur is celebrated with a feast and with people visiting one another, asking for forgiveness for wrongs committed against one another during the year. In the Jewish faith, one cannot go to God for forgiveness until one receives forgiveness from those one hurt. No work is done on Yom Kippur. In Jesus' time, people would take an animal to the temple to be sacrificed. Jesus would have participated in these events his entire life. Jesus is often referred to as a "lamb" to be sacrificed by spilling his own blood to atone for our sins. To atone often involves sacrifice, forgiveness, and mercy. We seek it, and we are asked to give it.

START THINKING

Look at the following list and assign a physical "weight" to each item. Use words like "boulder," "truck," "anvil," "free weight," and so on.

I lied to my parents. _____

I cheated on a test. _____

I let someone else cheat off my test. _____

I forgot to pick up my little sister from her after-school class.

_____

I was so angry, I wished someone dead. _____

I used the Lord's name in vain. _____

I spent the money that was supposed to go in the offering plate.

_____

I cheated on my boyfriend/girlfriend. _____

I skipped church because I was out late the night before.

_____

I slept through church because I was out late the night before.

_____

TABLE NOTES

In the space below or on a napkin or the back of a place mat, draw a box. Any size. Any shape. Give it some weight.

Now list ten ways you can make that box lighter.

SCRIPTURE MENU

Look up one or more of the sets of verses, and respond to the discussion questions that follow.

Romans 3:21–26 (NRSV)

21But now, irrespective of law, the righteousness of God has been disclosed, and is attested by the law and the prophets, 22the righteousness of God through faith in Jesus Christ for all who believe. For there is no distinction, 23since all have sinned and fall short of the glory of God; 24they are now justified by his grace as a gift, through the redemption that is in Christ Jesus, 25whom God put forward as a sacrifice of atonement by his blood, effective through faith. He did this to show his righteousness, because in his divine forbearance he had passed over the sins previously committed; 26it was to prove at the present time that he himself is righteous and that he justifies the one who has faith in Jesus.

Yom Kippur, though a day of fasting, is not about sacrifice but about reconciliation. Have you ever felt like you were "far" from yourself? What do you do to get it together?

Have you ever felt far from God?

What does it mean to be justified? How does that happen? More important, how do you remain justified?

Hebrews 1:3 (NRSV)

He is the reflection of God's glory and the exact imprint of God's very being, and he sustains all things by his powerful word. When he had made purification for sins, he sat down at the right hand of the Majesty on high....

Would Jesus ever come back? Do you think it could happen or is Jesus already a part of the "here and now"?

Ephesians 5:14-20 (NIV)

14For it is light that makes everything visible. This is why it is said:

**"Wake up, O sleeper,
rise from the dead,
and Christ will shine on you."**

¹⁵Be very careful, then, how you live--not as unwise but as wise, ¹⁶making the most of every opportunity, because the days are evil. ¹⁷Therefore do not be foolish, but understand what the Lord's will is. ¹⁸Do not get drunk on wine, which leads to debauchery. Instead, be filled with the Spirit. ¹⁹Speak to one another with psalms, hymns and spiritual songs. Sing and make music in your heart to the Lord, ²⁰always giving thanks to God the Father for everything, in the name of our Lord Jesus Christ.

Break this passage from Ephesians down into a two-word bumper sticker:

LIVE _____

Read Psalms 64 and 65 together.

Imagine that your "baggage" is really baggage. What does it look like? Is it a matching set of suitcases you can't carry alone? Is it a messenger bag with fraying straps and dripping something icky? Take a moment and then talk about your "baggage."

Read Hebrews 9:9–14.

TAKE HOME BAG

Look at your ten ways to make the box lighter you listed in Table Notes. Pick one of those ways, and think of that as an allegory for something you could do for someone else this week.

TIP

He deserves Paradise who makes his companions laugh.

—Qur'an

BOO

Theme: ALL HALLOWS' EVE

Order Here

Halloween is *not* about Spiderman costumes and "fun size" Snicker's bars. Halloween is *not* the devil's holiday. Any connection between Satan and All Hallows' Eve comes entirely from us and not the Bible.

Many, *many* years ago, the Druids would worship in cemeteries toward the end of summer and the beginning of autumn. The early church, when they laid out their calendar, would place their own holidays on the same days as many of the pagan holidays in an effort to bring others to God. The early church chose All Hallows' Eve and All Saints' Day to be in October/November. People believed that if you gathered in a cemetery to worship God you would be able to see the spirits of your departed loved ones rise up and go to heaven. It was a time of grief and remembrance. It was a time to look up the verses in the scriptures that talk about the dead coming to life and ghosts visiting the living. It was about God, not the devil.

Start Thinking

Number the following items 1 to 10 in order of their inherent goodness as far as Trick or Treat candies go, with 1 being the worst and 10 being the best.

Smarties

Apples

Fun-size Twix

Fun-size Peanut Butter Cups

Spider Rings

Pencils with "Happy Halloween" written on the side

Gum

M&M's

Edible eyeballs

Actual eyeballs

TABLE NOTES

In the space below, in your journal, or on the back of a place mat, draw a picture of your own headstone. Make it as detailed or as intricate as you want it to be.

SCRIPTURE MENU

Look up the verses and ask the questions that follow.

Read 1 Samuel 28:3–25.
Saul was about to have his butt handed to him in battle. He was scared and he wanted to find a fortune teller to tell him how things would go. Unfortunately he had had all of the fortune tellers put to death not long before this.

Do you believe in ghosts? Why and how?

Do you believe that the "soul" or "spirit" of a person can hang around after they are dead?

Many of the Jews of Jesus' time believed the spirit would hang around for up to three days. What would you do if you had three day to just "be" anywhere? Would you go to your own funeral?

Do you believe in fortune tellers and psychics?

Job 4:12–21 (MsgB)
"A word came to me in secret—
   a mere whisper of a word, but I heard it clearly.
It came in a scary dream one night,
   after I had fallen into a deep, deep sleep.
Dread stared me in the face, and Terror.
   I was scared to death—I shook from head to foot.
A spirit glided right in front of me—
   the hair on my head stood on end.
I couldn't tell what it was that appeared there—
   a blur...and then I heard a muffled voice:
'How can mere mortals be more righteous than God?
   How can humans be purer than their Creator?
Why, God doesn't even trust his own servants,
   doesn't even cheer his angels,
So how much less these bodies composed of mud,
   fragile as moths?
These bodies of ours are here today and gone tomorrow,
   and no one even notices—gone without a trace.
When the tent stakes are ripped up, the tent collapses—
   we die and are never the wiser for having lived.'"

Talk about a personal "ghost" story. When has something unexplained happened to you?

Why do you think ghosts and goblins hold such a fascination for people?

Read Ezekiel 37:1–14.

This story was most likely trying to make a bigger point about a people who had lost their way and were pretty much "dead" in the eyes of God. What calls us back when we have drifted? Answer that both personally and as part of a society.

What is God's promise to those who have lost their way?

Have you ever felt dead inside? When and why?

Matthew 27:51–53 (NRSV)

⁵¹At that moment the curtain of the temple was torn in two, from top to bottom. The earth shook, and the rocks were split. ⁵²The tombs also were opened, and many bodies of the saints who had fallen asleep were raised. ⁵³After his resurrection they came out of the tombs and entered the holy city and appeared to many.

Why isn't this passage from Matthew a big part of the Easter story? What would our Easter traditions look like if it were? Have you ever seen one of George Romero's "Dead" movies?

Some churches refuse to have Halloween parties and instead go for the "Autumnal Festivals." Other churches try to create "Hell House" type experiences to scare "the devil" out of teens and get them to commit to Jesus. How does your church view Halloween? What happens when you get scared into something?

TAKE HOME BAG

Who was the person close to you who most recently passed away? Write that person's name down here.

Now choose one of these Psalms: 13, 103, 108, 143, or 130. This week, take time and think about the person whose name you wrote down and use any of the Psalms as your evening prayer.

All unwittingly, Mr. Orson Welles and the Mercury Theater of the Air have made one of the most fascinating and important demonstrations of all time. They have proved that a few effective voices, accompanied by sound effects, can convince masses of people of a totally unreasonable, completely fantastic proposition as to create a nationwide panic.

—Dorothy Thompson, in 1938 on the day after Orson Welles broadcast

"War of the Worlds," quoted in **The New York Times**

COME ON RISE UP

THEME: ALL SAINTS' DAY

ORDER HERE

The celebration known as All Saints' Day—also called the Festival of All Saints or simply All Saints—has been celebrated in Western Christian culture since about the year 609. It was established by Pope Gregory and has undergone a number of changes but it is essentially the same. Think of All Saints as a sort of Christian Veteran's Day when we honor all the Saints known and unknown. There is a belief called The Communion of Saints, in which *all* God's people living and dead are connected through communion. All Saints is a celebration recognizing that everything that God created is connected to everything else.

START THINKING

Score each of the statements below on a scale of "connectivity," with 1 meaning "not even close" and 10 meaning "connected and charging!"

How connected are you to...

- The woman at the next table (if you're in a café)
- The story of the chair you're sitting on
- Your teachers

- Your graduation from high school
- Your parents
- Your grandparents
- Your great grandparents
- The members of your confirmation class
- The minister who baptized you
- The world itself
- God
- Jesus
- The Holy Spirit

TABLE NOTES

On a napkin, the back of a place mat, or another sheet of paper, create a connect-the-dots game for the person who is sitting across from you. When you have finished, switch papers.

SCRIPTURE MENU

Look up one or more of the sets of verses, and respond to the discussion questions that follow.

Read 1 Corinthians 1:1–3.

Paul expands his greeting to everyone, everywhere, whether they profess a faith or not. Everyone is a saint and worthy of being treated as such. What would your high school look like if everyone treated everyone else as a saint? What makes that notion sound absurd?

Do you believe that certain people are set aside as "more holy" than others? Can you name some of those people? Paul says that the "gifts and benefits" of being "set aside" belong to everyone, not just "the holy ones." Do you see that as a warning or an invitation or something else entirely?

Read 1 Corinthians 2:14–16.

Who are the "unspiritual" people in your life? What is their function? Have you ever asked "Isaiah's question" in verse 16? If Christ knows, is he sharing? Explain.

Ephesians 1:17–19 (NRSV)

[17]I pray that the God of our Lord Jesus Christ, the Father of glory, may give you a spirit of wisdom and revelation as you come to know him, [18]so that, with the eyes of your heart enlightened, you may know what is the hope to which he has called you, what are the riches of his glorious inheritance among the saints, [19]and what is the immeasurable greatness of his power for us who believe, according to the working of his great power.

We become saints when we say, "I'm going to live this way. I'm going to live and be the best person I possibly can."

Have you ever been in a large group of people all singing or dancing or cheering? What stops us from living each day like this? What breaks down the connection between us?

Read Ephesians 4:15–16.

Read Hebrews 12:1–3.

The Catholic Church believes in Patron Saints—beings who were once human and now intercede between us and heaven. You don't have to believe in "saints" like that, but do you believe that there is some sort of beings of God that reside on earth? Why or why not?

Take Home Bag

Ephesians 6:18 (MsgB)
In the same way, prayer is essential in this ongoing warfare. Pray hard and long. Pray for your brothers and sisters. Keep your eyes open. Keep each other's spirits up so that no one falls behind or drops out.

In the space below or on a napkin or the back of a place mat, write down five ways you can be "saintly."

Tip

And shepherds we shall be, for Thee, my Lord, for Thee. Power hath descended forth from Thy hand, that our feet may swiftly carry out Thy command. So we shall flow a river forth to Thee, and teeming with souls shall it ever be.

—*Billy Connelly as Il Duce in* **The Boondock Saints**

LAMPS

Theme: HANUKKAH (CHANUKAH)

Order Here

Hanukkah is not the "Jewish Christmas." It is not connected with Christmas in any way other than its proximity to Christmas on the calendar. Hanukkah is the Festival of Lights in which Jewish people celebrate the rededication of the Temple of Jerusalem.

After taking back the Temple from the Syrians, the Jewish people wanted to rededicate the Temple, but it had been trashed by the armies that had occupied it. The Jews wanted the Temple ready by the Sabbath but that would require working through the night for eight nights. They had enough oil to burn in the lamps for only one night. Yet, the lamps burned for eight—it was a miracle. The lighting of the lights is still celebrated with a special candle holder called a menorah. The menorah may only be used during the celebration of Hanukkah.

Start Thinking

Imagine you have a dimmer switch. Rate each of the following on a scale of brightness, with 1 meaning "in the dark" and 10 meaning "I gotta wear shades."

- My future
- My past
- Trigonometry

- Shakespeare
- God's plan
- The Bible
- The opposite sex
- The Electoral College
- College applications

TABLE NOTES

In the space below or on a separate sheet of paper, draw eight candles (unlit). On each candle write a few letters to represent some places in your life where things are unclear or "in the dark" or simply worrying you.

If light brings "illumination," which candle would you want to light first? What happens when you light one candle in a room full of unlit candles?

Explain one of your unlit candles with the rest of the table. Everyone can then offer an idea that will help light the light.

SCRIPTURE MENU

Read or look up one or more of the verses, and respond to the discussion questions that follow.

There are three blessings said on the first night of Hanukkah. Only two are said the following nights. Here they are in Hebrew as well as English.

First Blessing
Barukh ata Adonai Eloheinu melekh ha olam, she hehiyanu v'kiy'manu v'higi'anu la z'man ha ze.

Blessed are You, LORD, our God, King of the universe, who has kept us alive, sustained us, and enabled us to reach this season.

The first blessing is read only on the first night of Hanukah. What three things does this blessing recognize?

What is the difference between sustaining and keeping alive?

Answer the questions below for your own life.

God keeps me alive. How?

God sustains me. With what?

God enables me. For what purpose?

Second Blessing
Barukh ata Adonai Eloheinu melekh ha olam, asher kid'shanu b'mitzvotav vetzivanu l'hadlik ner (shel) hanuka.
Blessed are You, LORD, our God, King of the universe, who has sanctified us with His commandments and commanded us to light the Hanukkah candle[s].

In the second blessing God has sanctified us with his commandments. What does it mean to sanctify something? How can God's instructions do that?

What symbols of faith do we have in our religion that God called on us to do?

Third Blessing
Barukh ata Adonai Eloheinu melekh ha-olam, she asa nisim la avoteinu ba-yamim ha heim ba z'man ha ze.
Blessed are you, LORD, our God, King of the universe, who performed miracles for our ancestors in those days at this time.

Notice that in all three blessings there is no request for more blessings or for a bright future. Each one is about the past and how it brought us here. Can you think of an event in your past that made you who you are? It doesn't have to be complicated or major. Just something that happened "then" that helped make you who you are "now."

Genesis 1:3–5 (NRSV)
[3]**Then God said, "Let there be light"; and there was light.** [4]**And**

God saw that the light was good; and God separated the light from the darkness. ⁵God called the light Day, and the darkness he called Night. And there was evening and there was morning, the first day.

Maybe God didn't like to work in the dark. Do you think it is significant that the first thing we learn of God calling for is light? Why?

Read Psalm 18:28, Psalm 18:28, andMatthew 5:14–15.

What do you notice about these three texts?

When was the last time someone was "dark" to you?

Who was the last person who was a "light" to your darkness?

Take Home Bag

One light makes it easier to light other lights. When that one light goes out, it becomes hard to get the others lit. Growth makes growing easier. Love makes loving easier. Faith makes faith easier.

Think of the ways in Table Notes that others suggested to you to help light your lights. This week, help light someone else's candle.

Put on your yarmulke,
Here comes Hanukkah!
So much funukah,
To celebrate Hanukkah!
Hanukkah is the festival of lights.
Instead of one day of presents,
We have eight crazy nights.

—Adam Sandler

DO NOT OPEN TILL CHRISTMAS

THEME: ADVENT

ORDER HERE

The word "Advent" comes to us from the Latin word for "arrival" or "expectation." When you were little, did you ever stand at the window waiting for someone to arrive, as if your being there would make it happen sooner? That's the feeling of Advent. Advent usually starts on the Sunday closest to November 30 and lasts through Christmas Eve.

START THINKING

How well do you wait? Rank the following from 1 to 10, with 1 meaning "doesn't bug me" and 10 meaning "I can't stand it!"

- The night before Christmas
- The night before vacation
- The night before the first day of school
- Waiting for your food at a restaurant
- Waiting for the movie to start in a theater
- Waiting for the sermon to be over
- Waiting for a traffic light to turn green
- Waiting for your computer to boot up

TABLE NOTES

Many churches use an Advent wreath as part of the season. The meaning attributed to the four candles can vary depending on the denomination and, sometimes, the church. But typically the candle on the third Sunday represents Joy. As you did for Hanukkah, draw four unlit candles.

Let us imagine that these are the candles of Expectation, Simplicity, Joy, and Peace. Apply each of these names to one of your four candles. "Light" the one that seems be the focus of your life right now. Which one is giving you the most trouble?

SCRIPTURE MENU

Look up the verses and ask the questions that follow.

The following verses all take place before Jesus was born. The first few are the words of the prophets, and the others are about people that Jesus actually knew.

Isaiah 7:14 (MsgB)
So the Master is going to give you a sign anyway. Watch for this: A girl who is presently a virgin will get pregnant. She'll bear a son and name him Immanuel (God-With-Us).

Micah 5:2 (NRSV)
But you, O Bethlehem of Ephrathah,
 who are one of the little clans of Judah,
from you shall come forth for me

one who is to rule in Israel,
whose origin is from of old,
  from ancient days.

Zechariah 12:10 (NRSV)

And I will pour out a spirit of compassion and supplication on the house of David and the inhabitants of Jerusalem, so that, when they look on the one whom they have pierced, they shall mourn for him, as one mourns for an only child, and weep bitterly over him, as one weeps over a firstborn.

Jeremiah 31:15 (ESV)

Thus says the Lord: "A voice is heard in Ramah, lamentation and bitter weeping. Rachel is weeping for her children; she refuses to be comforted for her children, because they are no more."

Each of these first four passages has a corresponding event in the New Testament. Do you think the authors of the New Testament had "fulfilling" in mind when they wrote?

Do we still have prophets today?

What is meant by the phrase "Prophesy is not prediction"?

Would you want to know what's coming even if it were tragic?

Prophecy would allow us to prepare but not to prevent. If stories of "something wonderful" and of "something tragic" had been passed down in your family, school, and church for generations, how much would "preparation" be a part of your life and culture?

Matthew 1:18–21 (NRSV)

[18]Now the birth of Jesus the Messiah took place in this way. When his mother Mary had been engaged to Joseph, but before they lived together, she was found to be with child from the Holy Spirit. [19]Her husband Joseph, being a righteous man and unwilling to expose her to public disgrace, planned to dismiss her quietly. [20]But just when he had resolved to do this, an angel of the Lord appeared to him in a dream and said, "Joseph, son of David, do not be afraid to take Mary as your wife, for the child conceived in her is from the Holy Spirit. [21]She will bear a son, and you are to name him Jesus, for he will save his people from their sins."

Joseph often gets overlooked in all this, but he made some major sacrifices and took a whole lot on faith. Would you want the job of "stepdad" to the Messiah? Explain.

In that time, an unmarried pregnant girl would have been stoned to death. If your best friend or girlfriend said, "I'm pregnant and it's God's baby," what would it take for you honestly to believe her? Have you ever had a dream that was so real it was scary?

Where did your name come from? Do you know what it means?

Luke 1:11–20 (NRSV)

[11]**Then there appeared to him an angel of the Lord, standing at the right side of the altar of incense.** [12]**When Zechariah saw him, he was terrified; and fear overwhelmed him.** [13]**But the angel said to him, "Do not be afraid, Zechariah, for your prayer has been heard. Your wife Elizabeth will bear you a son, and you will name him John.** [14]**You will have joy and gladness, and many will rejoice at his birth,** [15]**for he will be great in the sight of the Lord. He must never drink wine or strong drink; even before his birth he will be filled with the Holy Spirit.** [16]**He will turn many of the people of Israel to the Lord their God.** [17]**With the spirit and power of Elijah he will go before him, to turn the hearts of parents to their children, and the disobedient to the wisdom of the righteous, to make ready a people prepared for the Lord."** [18]**Zechariah said to the angel, "How will I know that this is so? For I am an old man, and my wife is getting on in years."** [19]**The angel replied, "I am Gabriel. I stand in the presence of God, and I have been sent to speak to you and to bring you this good news.** [20]**But now, because you did not believe my words, which will be fulfilled in their time, you will become mute, unable to speak, until the day these things occur."**

Does the angel's reaction seem a little harsh?

Would you rather be the candidate at the mic accepting the nomination on camera or that "elbow" just off screen belonging to the person who got the nominee there?

We say, "Nothing is impossible with God," but how much do we really believe it?

The time leading up to Jesus' birth is full of angels and announcements. What has been the biggest "event" in your life so far? What's coming soon? How do you let people know?

What was the last thing hyped on TV and elsewhere that ultimately disappointed you? (A CD release? A summer blockbuster?)

How do you prepare for something so big you have no idea how to prepare for it appropriately?

TAKE HOME BAG

Look at the candles you drew in Table Notes. Choose one of the remaining three candles, "light" it, and give it to someone who needs it.

TIP

It is the beautiful task of Advent to awaken in all of us memories of goodness and thus to open doors of hope.

—John Cardinal Ratzinger (now Pope Benedict XVI)

NO ROOM

Theme: CHRISTMAS

Order Here

"And at that time there went forth a decree from Caesar Augustus...." So begins what many people consider to be the greatest story ever told. They are words we have heard so many times we recognize them right away. They fill us with memories of Christmases past and remind us of why we're in this to begin with. Christmas celebrates the birth of Jesus—God's son on earth or God in human flesh or the greatest educator who ever lived. Whatever your belief, whatever your question, there has never been a single individual who has changed the world more than this one.

Start Thinking

Rank the following on a scale of 1 to 10 according to the level at which it all connects and "becomes" Christmas to you.

- The first snowfall
- The children's Christmas pageant
- Putting up the tree
- Hearing carols on the radio
- Hearing carols at the mall
- My first taste of candy canes
- My first taste of Starbucks' pumpkin latte
- The candles on Christmas Eve
- Opening presents
- Hearing the Christmas story read in church
- Watching "A Charlie Brown Christmas"

TABLE NOTES

Mary gets the Magnificat and the pretty solos in all the Christmas pageants. In the space below or on a separate sheet of paper, write some lines for Joseph.

SCRIPTURE MENU

Look up one or more of the sets of verses, and respond to the discussion questions that follow.

Read these four passages together.

Hebrews 2:9

Philippians 2:5-8

John 1:14 1

Peter 3:18

These four passages are about incarnation. What is "incarnation"? It may be hard to believe. The most brilliant theologians in the world have argued about this for centuries. Add your own brilliant theological ideas to the universe

Luke 2:1–20 (NRSV)

¹n those days a decree went out from Emperor Augustus that all the world should be registered. ²This was the first registration and was taken while Quirinius was governor of Syria. ³All went to their own towns to be registered. ⁴Joseph also went from the town of Nazareth in Galilee to Judea, to the city of David called Bethlehem, because he was descended from the house and family

of David. ⁵He went to be registered with Mary, to whom he was engaged and who was expecting a child. ⁶While they were there, the time came for her to deliver her child. ⁷And she gave birth to her firstborn son and wrapped him in bands of cloth, and laid him in a manger, because there was no place for them in the inn.

⁸In that region there were shepherds living in the fields, keeping watch over their flock by night. ⁹Then an angel of the Lord stood before them, and the glory of the Lord shone around them, and they were terrified. ¹⁰But the angel said to them, "Do not be afraid; for see—I am bringing you good news of great joy for all the people: ¹¹to you is born this day in the city of David a Savior, who is the Messiah, the Lord. ¹²This will be a sign for you: you will find a child wrapped in bands of cloth and lying in a manger." ¹³And suddenly there was with the angel a multitude of the heavenly host, praising God and saying,

¹⁴"Glory to God in the highest heaven,
and on earth peace among those whom he favors!"

¹⁵When the angels had left them and gone into heaven, the shepherds said to one another, "Let us go now to Bethlehem and see this thing that has taken place, which the Lord has made known to us." ¹⁶So they went with haste and found Mary and Joseph, and the child lying in the manger. ¹⁷When they saw this, they made known what had been told them about this child; ¹⁸and all who heard it were amazed at what the shepherds told them. ¹⁹But Mary treasured all these words and pondered them in her heart. ²⁰The shepherds returned, glorifying and praising God for all they had heard and seen, as it had been told them.

Have you heard this story every year of your life since you were born? Do you know anyone who has never heard this story?

Why do we use a crèche?

As discussed Exploration 2, the wise men did not show up at Jesus' door until he was three or four. What would happen if we took the three wise men out of the play? Or took the crèche out?

The first Christmas pageant (as far as we can tell) was led by Saint Francis and used adults and live animals in a parade. Talk about a pageant experience you've had.

What would be an equivalent of a "shepherd" in our culture? Why would God send the angels to appear to them?

Take Home Bag

Sometime before Christmas, read this wonderful, simple, and beautiful story aloud to someone else—in church, at a shelter, in the hospital, in a nursing home, to a small child...anywhere, to anyone. Just find a pair of listening ears and read the story aloud.

Tip

And that's what Christmas is all about, Charlie Brown.

—*Linus van Pelt*

AFTERWORD: HOW TO USE THIS BOOK

This book was born out of a conversation with a friend of mine at a large church in the central United States. She said that her church was going to do away with the traditional Sunday night meetings because of low attendance. They would keep Sunday morning as well as the Wednesday night Bible study. "The thing is," she said, "I still have fifty kids in and out of my office during the week, and it's not necessarily the same kids. What I need is a curriculum that requires no preparation—and that I can grab off my shelf, take four youth, and say 'Let's go over to Starbucks.'"

This book works two ways. The first is as an impromptu discussion starter to be used with five or less youth crammed into a booth at your favorite coffee shop or diner. The participants can write on place mats or napkins. Just you, a Bible (or a few, different versions), and a couple of pens, and you're ready to go.

You can also use this book as part of an on-going curriculum. If possible, give each participant his or her own copy of this book to write in and doodle on as a journal. If youth are sharing copies, it would be great if each youth could get his or her own journal, one that's small enough to fit into a book bag and be re-read or worked on at home.

Adapt It Up
Every youth worker has opened a book of games or discussions only to be faced with the first line, "Break your group into smaller groups of eight"—and you have a total of only six teens in the room. We've all had to "adapt it down" and try to make a large-group activity fit with a small group. This book is written so that a youth minister or Sunday school teacher can adapt it *up* for use with a larger group.

How to Use This Book
Each exploration is broken into six smaller sections. The activities can be followed sequentially or not.

Order Here
This is the introduction. You can read it aloud to your youth, or, if each has his or her own book, you can have them read along silently before moving on.

Start Thinking
These are quick focusing questions to get kids' brains in the proper mindset and the discussion moving. They are mostly fun questions, meant to start things off. There are no right or wrong answers, so pay attention to the responses. If possible, ask more questions based on the answers you receive. These answers will give you a good idea of where the discussion wants to go.

Table Notes

This section encourages active participation. Youth are asked to make lists, draw pictures, and so on. Make sure they know they don't have to be artists or poets to properly participate. Sometimes discussion is easier if your hands are busy, so encourage doodling—yes, in the books! The idea is to get teens to open up and talk about what they are thinking.

Scripture Menu

Encourage your youth to bring their own Bibles. Tell them they can go out and buy a translation that speaks to them (the more variety, the better). Be open to the idea of letting participants mark and write in their Bibles—to really use the books.

This section offers up several different scriptures. Use as many as you want. Each scripture reference is followed by one, two, or several discussion questions. This time may be when you have the deepest discussion and when participants may start asking their own questions. Pay attention to these and follow their logic—this book should be merely the starting point for deeper things. The goal is to help youth learn who they are and what they think and believe, and then to share that with others.

Take Home Bag

This section is a work-at-home assignment. If your participants each have their own books, this will be easier. If they don't, let them write down the assignment on the back of a place mat or napkin. If you are using this book as part of a regular gathering, tell participants that they don't have to share their answers unless they are comfortable doing so.

Tip

The tip is a quick "big idea" for the day, like a fortune in a cookie or the memorable quote on the side of the paper coffee cup. Encourage participants to see the tip as a life hint and to pay attention to how often it comes into play during the week.

The questions in this book have been around for ages. They are part of an attempt to explain our place in the universe. They are also questions that have inflamed many arguments and caused great schisms and separations in families and churches. It has been said that the job of the clergy is not to answer the questions but to protect them. Some things we won't know about God until we can pose the question face to face. In the meantime, this book is written to create discussion. If you don't come to a conclusion...just enjoy the ride.

Everyone likes to work with little kids. Their hugs are freely given, and they act like they are glad to see you. Finding leaders for the adult education program is a little harder, mostly because adults don't think they're smart enough to lead a Bible discussion. In adult classes you can have adult discussions, but you have chosen to work with teenagers. God bless you. I hope these books make you even better at what you do.